I'm Going To READ!™

These levels are meant only as guides;
you and your child can best choose a book that's right.

Level 1: Kindergarten–Grade 1 . . . Ages 4–6
- word bank to highlight new words
- consistent placement of text to promote readability
- easy words and phrases
- simple sentences build to make simple stories
- art and design help new readers decode text

Level 2: Grade 1 . . . Ages 6–7
- word bank to highlight new words
- rhyming texts introduced
- more difficult words, but vocabulary is still limited
- longer sentences and longer stories
- designed for easy readability

Level 3: Grade 2 . . . Ages 7–8
- richer vocabulary of up to 200 different words
- varied sentence structure
- high-interest stories with longer plots
- designed to promote independent reading

Level 4: Grades 3 and up . . . Ages 8 and up
- richer vocabulary of more than 300 different words
- short chapters, multiple stories, or poems
- more complex plots for the newly independent reader
- emphasis on reading for meaning

LEVEL 2

Library of Congress Cataloging-in-Publication Data Available

2 4 6 8 10 9 7 5 3 1

Published by Sterling Publishing Co., Inc.
387 Park Avenue South, New York, NY 10016
Text copyright © 2005 by Harriet Ziefert Inc.
Illustrations copyright © 2005 by Sanford Hoffman
Distributed in Canada by Sterling Publishing
c/o Canadian Manda Group, 165 Dufferin Street
Toronto, Ontario, Canada M6K 3H6
Distributed in Great Britain and Europe by Chris Lloyd at Orca Book
Services, Stanley House, Fleets Lane, Poole BH15 3AJ, England
Distributed in Australia by Capricorn Link (Australia) Pty. Ltd.
P.O. Box 704, Windsor, NSW 2756, Australia

I'm Going To Read is a trademark of Sterling Publishing Co., Inc.

Sterling ISBN 1-4027-2079-3

Good Dog, Rover

Pictures by Sanford Hoffman

Sterling Publishing Co., Inc.
New York

My name is Andy.
My sister's name
is Amy.

We are going to
adopt a dog.

Mom says,
"I don't like
little dogs."

Amy wants
a little dog.
I want
a big dog.

Dad says,
"I don't like
big dogs."

Amy says, "I don't
like black dogs."

I say, "I don't
like white dogs."

We go to the pound.
We look at lots and lots of dogs.

Little dogs . . .

big dogs . . .

white dogs . . .

and black dogs.

And then . . .

. . . we find Rover!

Rover is not big.
He is not little.
He is not white.
He is not black.
He's just right!

not   just   he   find

Rover likes us.

We like Rover.

So we take him home.

Rover is smart.
We teach him a trick.

"Good dog!"
"Good dog!"

I teach Rover
another trick . . .

and another . . .

and another!

"Good dog, Rover!"

At dinner Rover
shows us his tricks.

"No, Rover!"
"Get down!"
"Bad dog!"

Rover eats dinner.
"Not so fast, Rover!
Slow down!"

Later, Amy and I get
ready for bed.

"I want Rover to sleep
on my bed," says Amy.

"I want Rover to sleep
on my bed," I say.

can   in

"Rover can sleep
in his own bed,"
Mom and Dad say together.

Good dog, Rover.